# RATTLE OF THE WIND

# Rattle of the Wind

Darren Briggs

*San Francisco, California*

ISBN: 979-8-9921594-9-3

Cover artwork by Ed Musante

Author photo by Erin Briggs

*San Francisco, California*

*Faith is the bird that feels the light*
*when the dawn is still dark.*

—Rabindranath Tagore

*I prefer the absurdity of writing poems*
*to the absurdity of not writing poems.*

—Wisława Szymborska

*Let it come, as it will, and don't be afraid.*
*God does not leave us comfortless,*
*so let evening come.*

—Jane Kenyon

*For Erin*
*And for our children, Lindsey, David and Kelsey,*
*And our grandsons, Colten and Nash*

# CONTENTS

## IN THE DARK

The power has been off for three days. We stare
at each other in flickering candlelight, waiting
for the universe to fall back into place. Our
words threaten to spill over like a flood. Driven
by the wind and pulled by the moon, there is an
ocean at our doorstep. Everything stretched out
before us, like this patchwork quilt. Maybe we're
just afraid of uncertainty, maybe we'll feel different
when the rain stops. The past always plagues the
present, but our youth burned with its own beauty.
What's the point, you may ask, but weathering the
storm binds me to you forever. The lights come on
at 9:00 p.m.

## A LIMINAL MOMENT

I babble and superfluous words
spill out in a stammer. The thread
of the story escapes me, somewhere
between midnight and dawn.

I stand on a threshold, unmoored
from the present, removed from
the past. Where are my corroborators,
like leaves on the forest floor?

What's the difference between soul
and spirit, right and wrong, zeros
and ones? Life loses significance,
changes shape after dark.

It's not where everything goes, but
appears so connected. A stranger
recites prayer from memory,
I walk circles in this labyrinth.

Words frame the silence, as footsteps
echo hollow in an empty space. It's like
the pretense of a dream. I covet
the exquisite ordinariness.

What was once lovely is now scorched
and parched land. No matter how veritable
the abyss, morning comes early, a reticent
sunrise grows more lucent in the East.

## THE DISTANCE

A hesitant sunrise,
hours away and God
is a stranger.

When a thousand reversals
threaten setback at any
given moment.

Untethered from narrative,
left to our own
unfiltered words.

We send out these soundings,
only to hear them echo—
in our bodies.

Maybe there's no such thing
as closure, we just swim against
currents of ambivalent loss.

While the distance between us
is measured by all the words
we didn't say.

## WORLDS COLLAPSE

She kisses him absently
on New Year's Eve—
her eyes never so vacant.

Lights flicker,
the room fades,
time spills like a secret.

Moonlight stumbles,
stars fall like confetti,
planets twirl about the floor.

In an ever-eclipsing play,
worlds fall apart,
disintegrate, collapse.

## THIS YEAR IN STASIS

In this disassembled
landscape, once again
winter brings
despair.

Yet this blazing sky
in all its glory
still rests
upon the Earth—

on our peace
and disorder,
faith and doubt,
on life and death,

between our becoming
and undoing,
love and loss,
security and fear.

Winter ignores
our expectations,
it is only
here and now.

## EMPYREAN BLUE

I listen closely
to whispers and sighs.

Vibrant and variegated,
these windswept skies.

I let the winds carry me,
as leaves swirl and spin.

Gusts and drafts,
I ride the wind.

Just a movement of air,
I soar and glide.

The meeting place of gods,
these empyrean skies.

## WINTERING

It's coldest just before the dawn,
morning reveals a blanket
of immaculate white. A storm
has left you prepossessing,
unpredictable, holy.

The low brumal sun illuminates
the trees, thin shadows stretch
long through snow covered
branches. Blue light scatters
over sculpted snowdrifts.

The creek has frozen over,
blades of grass peek through
the powder. Much of life stays
hidden beneath the surface,
needed solace for the days after.

The imminent cold
of an enchanted season,
I have not loved you enough—
from the winter solstice
to the vernal equinox.

I lean into the wind, push
forward to the resurrection
of days, where new life blooms
against setback, with no
particular distress.

## GHOSTS

I dreamed I stood
in a flicker of light
on a landing between
two dark rooms.

I balked at moving,
unable to turn back.
I fully expected to see
you in the next instant.

Shuddered to think
you were lost,
a clinging leaf
riven by the wind.

Somehow, I knew
ghosts would inhabit
the hollows
my grief had left.

## DARKLY BEAUTIFUL

Evening pulses
with desire,
a strange confluence
of fire and water.

Seduced by the color,
as muted shades
of nightfall settle
around us.

A detailed topography,
darkly beautiful,
only shadow hides
its secrets.

Caught in the undertow—
the ocean claims us.
We are the crashing wave,
and the outgoing tide.

## EVIDENCE

All day, I carry words I cannot say,
and with the nearness of nightfall
my heart falters. Sometimes the
disjunction between what I hope
for, and what really happens
flutters like a bird inside my chest.

Despite my better efforts,
the gap between where I am,
and where I imagined I'd be,
expands into a thing that looks
more like evidence.

Some distances are never meant
to be passed over quickly. I've
learned to reserve judgement
and wait for the golden hour,
when light resolves, and
coalesces in trees.

Something shifts, a warmth that
comforts, a recognition maybe—
the kind that makes you breathe
deeper and exhale slowly.
Memories are not forgotten,
but may lose their power.

## MY ANTINOMIAN HEART

Their words of faith loose and
unleash something, like seeds
that scatter in the wind. A belief
in my own fiction, resistant to
the sincerest prayer. There are
irreducible complexities, and
a wilderness at the edge of all
understanding. I want to live
a life that feels like living, with
style, tireless attention, and
ideas that both mock and inspire.
I find virtue in equanimity.
Consider the trickle of a stream,
the lift that comes when birds
sing. Stand in a grove of oak
trees. Know you have love and
are loving. These consecrated
moments between the things
that are real and those that imitate.
I can divide my life on either side
of this line. I say, "More Life."
They say, "No Excess!" Cut off
the branches, settle for the golden
ending. Wear a peaceful expression
of the dead as the dwindling
congregation sings, *Just as I Am.*

## WINTER DARK

*For Erin Diane Briggs*

I stare as the winter
dark descends,
imagine the whole world
will never be enough.

Our eyes meet
in a nervous glance.
The melancholy is music.
It is a slow waltz,
a desperate dance.

I close my eyes to savor
this fugitive moment.
Implore you
with an open mouth kiss.
I whisper, I love you.

Your smile warmly recalls
an amused wistfulness,
maybe a reminiscence.
I am hopeful and breathless.

## RED UMBRELLA

Dark clouds threaten.
She dances barefoot,
twirls that red umbrella.
Me in clumsy rubber boots.

Light fades, fog blankets the
pavement. She glides through
the mist, pretends to kick and
splash. Her eyes flirt playful.

I laugh at her exuberance.
She always takes the lead, but
I gather her in, pull her close.
Rain falls in a downpour.

A flash of light and the boom
of thunder, that red umbrella on
the ground. Only my feet are dry.
Our lips wet with raindrops.

## THE DANCE

In cloistered darkness,
we close our eyes, imagine
ourselves the only ones
dancing, at this time, in this
town, anywhere. We pass
through moonbeams, patterns
on the bedroom floor, follow
a halting elliptical path, orbit
in and out of each other's reach,
in circular motion, with golden
thread, the rush of wind, words
of love and suffering often
interchangeable. We would
not be the same lovers, if not
for the dance.

## A MORNING WALK

takes me through a gravenstein apple
orchard, and into the woods. Startled by
my approach, two cottontails hurry into
a thicket of blackberries. I'm already
beginning to see the brambles flower.
It seems only a few months ago, I was
picking their fruit.

The croak of a bullfrog and the slow trickle
of water. Yesterday's rain has muddied
the path. Staring from a valley oak,
a red-shouldered hawk appears to follow me
as I make my way up the hillside. A family
of quail scramble, and the trees open to a
verdant meadow.

A blue bellied lizard sunbathes on a rock.
I lie down in the tall grass with the smell
of earth and the fragrance of wildflowers.
Lupines, goldenrod, irises, ladybugs,
butterflies, and so many bees.

Not a cloud in the sky, humid air rises
as the sun beats down. Overcome with
drowsiness, I close my eyes. The silence
gives way to a whisper and the intermittent
singing of a northern yellow warbler.

## HAWK AND CROW

I roost among avian
utterances, defoliated
branches, the clatter
of bones.

No line divides
joy from grief, no easy
binaries for anything
meaningful.

First-person epiphany,
freedom in uncertainty,
I live between hawk and crow,
each demands territory.

I cast off tired feathers,
explore new forms
and expressions, discard
old habits, attitudes, beliefs.

## ROCKS I STACK

I skirt the woods that
border the property and
walk along a fence line
in the shade of trees.

The underbrush is thick
with a musty decay. Early
November winds hint
of the coming snow.

I tilt my face to the sun
to track a gaggle of geese
overhead, and a heaviness
inside me lifts.

The commotion carries
on the cold morning air,
migration to their
overwinter home.

Ivory clouds reconstitute
in a condensation of
imagination. Small birds
dart between branches.

The rocks I stack look like
a headstone—maybe an altar.
In a whirlwind, leaves hover
just above the ground.

## THE NARCISSIST

She shares enough of her heart for his to sting. He shoots her a leveling glance and looks back at his phone. There is something else she says, and it gives him pause. The often ill-fated impulse to place meaning where it no longer exists. It all seems so inscrutable to him, her use of many words, where fewer would do. The hole in his heart was always there, she only illuminates its darkness. There is a shrill of laughter somewhere in the bar. He shifts in his chair to scan the room and catches the eye of a stranger. He raises his brow in recognition. He smiles benignly, unaware his glass is empty.

## LOVER'S MANTRA

Our love
ignites passion,
fills with anticipation,
insists on intimacy,
has no measure.

Our love
pulls down barriers,
throws open floodgates,
expands heart space,
stretches the mind.

Our love
sees inside a new wholeness,
releases a creative muse,
manifests beauty,
flows with cascading joy.

Our love
finds all things converge,
risks everything,
holds nothing back,
overcomes fear.

## JUST DRIVE

With winter in my bones,
yesterday's cold rain
turned me round somehow,
turned me round.

Lulled by the rhythm
of the windshield wipers.
Lost in deliberate dislocation.
I found myself driving—

halfway to the ocean,
daydreaming of persimmon trees,
with their graceful form
and ornamental fruit.

Webs of black branches
adorned with bright orange globes,
long after the leaves have fallen
and the first snow has dropped.

## WEIRDO

On my twelfth birthday, my family packed up the car and drove to the San Francisco Airport. While serious conversation took place upfront, I sat in the backseat. With eyes shut, I composed music in my head. There was no need for my transistor radio. I had a habit of tapping my teeth to drum a beat, while I hummed a rhythm. In this way, I blocked everything out. At the airport, caught up in crescendo I staggered off-balance. A shearing pain silenced the anthem, like the stark quiet after a turntable has crashed to the floor. My eyes welled up, I cradled my arm. My brother lashed out, “Knock it off weirdo!” He was embarrassed to stand next to me while our father boarded a flight to Vietnam. We watched the plane taxi down the tarmac, until it was in the air. We left the terminal, my arm still sore, but I wished my brother could have heard the music.

## INSCRUTABLE HEART

With contentment
there is a lightness.

Sadness carries a
heavy weight.

We leap with joy and
fall in anguish.

For all happiness,
there is much sorrow.

## SUMMER DRESS

Under the restless light,
with its long shadow
of memory,
I step back.

Every image,
those dark eyes,
the summer dress,
hair pushed behind
the ear.

Framed, caught
in a photograph.
Momentary
abstraction in
black and white.

All expectations, regrets
and dreams deferred.
A foggy distanceless day,
given its direction.

## THE PICTURE

Everything appears tilted.
The picture of her always needs
to be straightened, like the world
on its axis must be righted.

In want of balance, on that nail
in the wall, hangs from a wire,
swings free with every slam
of the door.

As if this house suffers an
earthquake every time he passes,
the picture frame off-kilter,
catches his eye.

All things askew require his
attention, "Up on the right, no,
the left, you've gone too far,
can't you do anything right?"

Her crooked mouth, a mocking
testament of how things become.
He demands she display a smile
on that face.

## DEEP WATER

The surface of her skin inclines
relative to the moonlight.

Notes of citrus and vanilla linger. Her
voice fills with counterfeit excitement.

A sea of hollow greens, evasive
blues, conceal the darkness.

She throws her head back
in laughter, aware of the deceit.

In the withdrawn silence,
there's a rustle of silk.

With a rise of the tide,
he finds himself in deep water.

Without promise of a future,
her words push him under.

## AFTER THE RAIN

After the rain, wind and sun
wrap the morning, though
more weather untenable
sorrow creates.

Under blue skies
a thousand wings flutter,
my harrowed heart
fragile as it is resilient.

The connection I feel
beneath the trees, as the years
pass these woodlands
grow emptier.

Afraid of a holy fear, in
search of fullness, my sense
of things shift with the telling
of the story.

Time bends or doubles back,
it may exist elsewhere, the line
blurs that demarcates before
and after.

All this distilled loveliness proves
nothing of considerable worth,
I mourn and muse in the event,
grief and happiness can coexist.

The painted sun has a faded
patina, *and I am waiting for a
rebirth of wonder*, with the notion
that even the dust is sacred.

## MOIRAI

A fated night
of restless dreams,
a fine-spun cloth,
unravels at length.
Scarcely cut off,
born of destiny,
the past, present
and future, collapse
the distance between
life and the certainty
of death.

## MORNING RITUAL

A hooded oriole
flashes orange, dives
into an elephant tree.

White-crowned sparrows
scatter, a startled
cactus wren lets loose
with a rattling call.

Between branches,
two hummingbirds
dance the conchero.

An iguana, unaware
of the blessing, crawls
from under an agave.

From sea to land,
the unabated surf
raises its hand
to soothe the shore.

## BY THE POOL

A narrow wind blows
off the water's surface,
her long legs cross,
feet dangling.

She tilts her head
to glimpse
over sunglasses,
wisps of hair waft
from beneath a hat.

He takes in the voluptuous
hypnotic sway of palm trees,
the corner of her mouth
betrays amusement.

She purses her lips
in a self-deprecating way,
and sips a mimosa.

The thought of touching
her skin—
makes him
incredibly unsettled.

## STORIES HE TELLS

He just dumps all his sadness into
a poem, dark and mirthless, often
filled with heartache.

It seems life has diminished him
with a cumulative effect, some things
he can never get back.

Speaks as if he understands, shows
up when least expected, the stories he
tells, always change significantly.

He laughs if things get tragic, a
pretender, a lover of songs, a religion
to himself.

Appears foolish, at other times wise.
He is a hero, a creator, a trickster—a villain
one moment, saves the day in the next.

He throws out those gnawing questions,
that create space to be misunderstood.
Chooses not to say what he means,

always leaves it to interpretation. And
at times, the profound pull of his power
seems to distort all efforts.

## LIKE A PEACH

*For Jessica Berry*

I wake with a
pounding heart
and the premonition
something's not
right. Life can be
hard, but like
a peach, the
first bite sends
juice running
down my chin,
the last bite may
break my teeth.
I question what
might happen,
in an attempt
to do something
different.

## BRUSHWORK

In a world of disenchantment,
the spirit grieves, but blank canvas

provides endless possibility. I paint
dark shadows, vibrations in the air.

Broad strokes, delicious embellishment,
hesitant light delineates boundary.

These fixings are the stories I tell myself.
While beauty awaits the unveiling,

I capture time—remember the warmth
of her breath on my lips.

## WHEN IN ROME

In the plaza, a vender sells gelato,
tourists walk through a flock of
pigeons like a parting of the Red Sea.

A street performer busks under
the shade of trees, music echoes
off the enduring architecture.

Lovers embrace, kiss as if life
depends on it, summer heat rises
off the pavement.

Crouched on the sidewalk, an olive
skinned boy paints a masterpiece
with chalk in bold Renaissance color.

An old man shouts at kids that weave
through the crowds on the hunt for
an exploitable mark.

Scattered clouds appear like cotton,
children run with delight, and birds
flutter in the wake of their passing.

We throw coins over our shoulders,
to ensure our return, pause for a
Japanese family as they take photos.

## A BREAK IN THE TREES

I look toward the meadow
from a break in the trees, I push
my way forward through
branches and leaves.

Sometimes when I stare
directly, I often fail to see,
I need to walk around it,
to see more vividly,

the rich and varied nuances,
yellows, browns, deep blues and
greens, between forest and the
meadow, under a border canopy.

Behind me, the forest seems
to rattle and to hum, the trees
are like an ocean, I hear
rhythm and the drums.

Wildflowers bloom,
grass wafts to and fro,
the field undulates, the
stalks bend low.

Aware of my presence, no
reason for them to fear, birds
cease their reticence, sing out
loud and clear.

The longer that I linger in
this solitude so sublime, my
spirit stilled and quiet, I lose
all sense of time.

The heavens reconcile,
swallows dip and glide,
clouds move in from the west
across the summery sky.

## FLOWERS FOR BEULAH

I count my steps in an exercise
of memory, as well as physical
well-being.

As a young boy I walked these
same rows, heedful not to trample
the graves.

Great-grandma and I carried
flowers, visited where our
loved ones rest.

I learned respect for the dead from
her silence—as she carefully placed
iris, columbine, and delphinium.

Her daughter, my father's mother,
my grandmother, buried years
before my birth.

I knew her only from family photos,
until reading the many poems
she wrote.

## AFTER AUGUST

In the retreating days of
summer, a red-shouldered
hawk ruffles its feathers,
zephyr winds blow, treetops
sweep the sky and acorns
fall in anticipation.

## PICTURES OF JUPITER

A painterly triumph,
mutable in its parts, when
it comes into focus we see
that it's art.

Theophany or apostasy,
on the spectrum of light,
spun in a mixer, cerulean
blue, marshmallow white.

This liquid confection,
cinnamon brown, Tyrian
purple in hue, Payne's grey
and some midnight blue.

A beautiful giant, what
secrets in store, lipstick
red, yellow ochre—
I want to see more.

A look at the surface,
another Starry Night,
Van Gogh was from Jupiter,
that explains it alright.

## BALANCING ACT

A hawk's piercing cry—
doing a balancing act,
in the tallest tree.

## AGAIN

Again, the air
was invisible. I was
blindly unaware, when love
vanishes, it becomes unbearable.

Again, the wind
a ceaseless howling.
Grief passes through me
like a ghost—languishing.

Again, the rain
a torrential downpour.
If only the flood recedes
before drowning.

Again, the cold
a black murmuration.
The vulnerable beauty of survival,
at best a requisite for moving forward.

## A TENDER MERCY

*For David Leon Zink*

For weeks, I've kept
watch on a bird's nest
in the wisteria, where
a mother bird fed her
helpless chicks, only
to find one dead on
the grass, the nest
abandoned. I often
question life's absurdity,
though God remains
silent. I wait for
something to cut
through the disorder,
haunted by the painful
shape of absence. I
never did trust happiness,
yet the appearance of
everything is altered.
My faith or lack of it
resolves in a deepening
gratitude. I still look
for the hidden beauty.

## LAZARUS RECLINING

Resuscitate the darkness,
parse the surface of the deep,
distinct from feelings that are
not immediately obvious.

Awareness isn't what I
understood in silence, it's what
remained when circumstances
became intransigent.

When the body betrays—
and illness threatens identity,
swept along, by *life's inevitable*
*contingency*.

Did I witness resurrection,
feel mountains tremble,
or hear weeping outside
the tomb?

I'm still looking for incremental
transformation, when there
is more light in my mind
then there is shadow.

A diminutive change
at the beginning can lead
to massive divergence
in the end.

The river runs in sinuous
surrender. There's no longer
any need to win, nor any
compulsion to dominate.

Silence intrudes and exerts
its weight, it's good to give
thanks, in the quiet space
between breath.

## INTO THE MYSTERY

*In memory of Terry Briggs*

A faint smell of jasmine,
all but imperceptible.
Before *the hour of shining stars*,
I walk.

I sense an unseen twining,
woven through days and seasons.
A condition of beauty, carried
forward at intervals.

I fix my eyes on the darkness
between the trees.
In wonderment I blink
away the afterimages.

Uncertain the world
will right itself,
true ambiguity seldom
rises above confusion.

I feel and hear the distance,
edge towards a waning light.
I sing like no one's listening,
as I dance into the mystery.

## MOCKINGLY

During the silent
spaces of night,
a mockingbird
sings incessantly.

Where trees darken,
and thick woods close in,
lie ghosts of words
that should never repeat.

Bring it back
to a place between
moments that have
no designation,

only impressions
of words that form
before they have time
to take shape.

String together imitations,
songs of different birds,
mimic others or sing
in a true voice,

like laughter at one's
own expense, deeper
compulsions scarcely
trusted to music.

## THE SHAPE OF THINGS

Is it grief that produces the
ghosts of those I've lost?
Do the dead gather, if I
never speak of them?

I keep listening to your voice
on saved phone messages.
My heart aches with every
commemorated loss.

How could you leave?
Your last appraisal of me
culminated in doubt, if not
something more serious.

This life, our possession
or its possession of us,
has left me fallow. Your
words an indelible mark.

What is the shape of things
to come? They can never be
the same.

## THE INJURY

If *geography is fate*, the landscapes and regions where we live and have lived, profoundly shape who we are and who we become. Beyond the contradictions and complexities, there is a subtle kind of violence that alters a place. For example, those new condominiums where that old Victorian house used to be, or when the city removed the juniper hedge that once encircled the park. Tragic are the days I drive past the local phone company and see their expanded facility instead of my grandparents' house. Sometimes, I walk up that street, because I can remember or recognize it by how it smells. These olfactory memories are like imprints that last undisturbed by later experience, and are often strong enough to transport me back through time. Knowing the former presence of that house, its erasure cuts through to the very heart of my childhood. The injury is one of history, a violation of autobiographic memory.

## WAR BY PROXY

Peace on earth… Don't we
make a sham of it? How soon
condemnation comes, and

we find ourselves in the thick
of it, the world is a stage,
we just can't resist

the posturing and theatrics,
the self-mythologizing need
to be blameless.

This terrible wind, cold
campaign tactics, devalues
the singularity of all others,

with willing suspension of
our disbelief we pretend
everything is replaceable,

whereas unique, remarkable,
incomparable lives are
reduced to a body count.

## MOLECULES

Molecules vibrate
at a higher frequency
when I am with you.

## THICK LIKE HONEY

*For Cindy Briggs*

Some things are weightless
as well as invisible, but harsh
words find their mark.

Balmy air feels thick like
honey, a suffocating
silence follows.

Eyes fix on the trees, fireflies
flicker and the woods blur
into indistinguishable color.

Blackness consumes the forest,
like a living thing, presses in
from all sides.

A clear, late summer evening
nonetheless, heavy with all
that is said.

## THE WAY LIGHT FALLS

We push our clocks
forward for another
hour of daylight,

notwithstanding the spin
of the planet, and cycle
of its circadian rhythm.

Parse the absurdity
of life's disappointments.
Try and fail, love and live.

When things fall apart,
another you, another me,
maybe another chance.

The slanting beauty
of words that excise
the entropy, the way

light falls through
trees and dapples
the forest floor.

## IN THE MIRROR

What maniacal
pleasure
the barber
seemed to take
at my expense.

My strength
and confidence
torpedoed
by another
military haircut.

I saw a different person
in that chair,
a stranger
leered
back at me.

A look of horror,
eyes filled
with sadness
and shattered
resignation.

A shadow of who
I wanted to be.
Tears
would not
be tolerated.

There could be
no flag
of rebellion
among
the ranks.

I had to pretend
to like it,
it was my duty,
I was
a naval officer's kid.

## BIRDS

Who would restrain,
or reduce their freedom?

Windows reflect magnolia
skies, expansive and
glorious as cathedrals.

It hit with a loud thunk,
a small smear spread
like oil on glass.

Broken, fallen—inert
on the solid ground.

How does one measure
such sorrow?

## READING KIERKEGAARD

An ever-changing play of
light and shadow, the world
I inhabit is not a home.

The attenuated darkness
of early morning, *sorrow on
the verge of revelation.*

With heavy stones I wade
into oblivion. The sensation
flickers like a vague memory.

Your knowledge of me
is gone, has left me
less than I had been.

My brain's ledger has an
indelible mark, the last entry
made with red ink.

## PERPETUAL WINTER

In the waste land,
where old stories lie
under new streets,

I am a ghost, anomalous,
cut off from life, neither
alive nor dead,

haunted, transplanted
in a mock world
I do not know.

With the tilt of the earth's axis,
winter calls, unspoken declarations
hover, never to land.

There is a still point at the center
of all movement, stillness proceeds
the dance.

Stillness in movement, movement
in stillness, silence in sound,
and sound in silence.

In the congregation
of shadows, I let reticence
be my agent.

Surrounded by roses,
the garden is where
I live and remain,

blood flows tumultuous,
the thrum of wings
in my head.

I've stopped rushing
into the future, every other
creature seems content.

The measure of joy
against all the torment,
still tilts the scales.

As the moon grows more
distant, life on the planet
will never be the same.

The tragedy of an august person
inevitably obscures the distress
of those who likewise suffer.

With no illusions… indeed, left
to my own devices, I destroyed
the very things I loved,

always the callow interloper,
pretending to be something else,
but now I am old.

I sit with the void, instead of trying
to fill it. Yet death comes gently,
my heart bound with steel.

## WHERE THE MIND GOES

*In memory of Marylane Briggs*

Gravity still
pulls and tugs,
most memories
remain untouched.

Interrogate the
darkness, slip out
of bed, wander
like a ghost,

across forest and
meadow, where it's
pleasant to see
the sun.

Cold shadows,
warm sunbeams,
reminders that
light is sweet.

## MORNING IS A RAVEN

Last night, I chased oblivion
and the beautiful. Morning
betrays me, leaves only
the vaguest impression.

Memory plays out in intervals,
discontinuous, shapeless,
like some imagined distance,
between then and now.

Unsettled, fleeting—
things I might have
written down, no longer
remembered.

I try to speak in present tense,
harder than one might expect,
intent on return to another
atmosphere altogether.

Dark wings gather, a chill,
penetrating wind blows through.
The smothering silence
further suggests I'm alone.

## THE DEVIL I KNOW

Some days life is like a book, I walk away
knowing every step and misstep. I guess
I could be like that guy who seems to live
by the motto, "fake it till you make it" in the
French novel, *Bel-Ami* or like Murakami's
protagonist in *South of the Border, West of
the Sun*, "a smelly old guy who is destined
to sleep on his couch."

There is a tension between acting and
observing, but there is condemnation if you
hesitate. Wendell Berry said, "The mystery
surrounding our life probably is not
significantly reducible. And so, the question
of how to act in ignorance is paramount."

My world is flat, like a list of places I'll never
visit. Life can be all subterfuge, deceit, or
passing oneself off as something one is not,
like Eliot's *Waste Land*, dissolving into
fleeting images in the ether.

Stories can turn tragic, like Kafka's man on
the bridge or akin to the real loss of James
Dean and Buddy Holly, ironically Albert
Camus told friends there would be nothing
more "absurd" than dying in a car crash.

I'm caught in this unending Russian novel
and I can't remember anyone's name. Maybe
I'm the idiot, one of the ordinary people, who
simply serve to propagate the species.
Certainly, not the extraordinary person who
must have "the right to transgress."

When I asked if you still loved me, you
never answered. I'm reminded of Sally
Rooney's, *Beautiful World*, "We are standing
in the last lighted room before the darkness…"
given that "there is no chance for the planet,
and no chance for us."

There's always Hemingway's famous line
about how a person goes bankrupt,
"Gradually and then suddenly." Every
self-loathing drinker knows this.

And as the sky grows darker around sunset,
time stops, Samuel Beckett says, "Fail again.
Fail better." My inner critic smiles wickedly,
and quips back like Hunter S. Thompson,
"You know you'll just fuck it up again!"

## NASCENT DREAMS

Silver clouds switch
passively over the cratered
surface. A wraithlike mist
sweeps into the yard.

Jupiter and a waning
gibbous moon steal across
the heavens, attendant over
hills and forests.

Nearby, the lovely,
ever-delicate Seven Sisters,
cosmic gems
of Taurus the Bull.

The fiery eye of Aldebaran,
set on the princess, her
soft glow quivers with
tremulous light.

Eyes half-open, my forehead
presses cold against the glass.
I tilt my head and linger
a few seconds longer.

## RATTLE OF THE WIND

I don't pray much
anymore. Maybe the
gods don't move me
like before.

The church has been
seduced, my love for her
is fallen, I still close my eyes
when birds are calling.

Is God still involved
with the things of man?
Is Jesus Democrat or
Republican?

Who am I to judge—
it's a foolish notion, when
I know so little about
extravagant devotion?

Will the rocks cry out
if I keep silent? Will I
die in triumphant
defiance?

Will I go out with joy, led
forth in peace, when
mountains burst into song
with all of the trees?

I try to forget you at least
twice a day, but the rattle
of the wind stirs me when
it sings in praise.

## OUTER AND INNER

He planted a vineyard slanted up to the skyline. New vines obliquely sown. He spoke elliptically. Indeed, how he danced around the subject. Withheld, when otherwise, he could have been more explicit. Yet not a refusal, the power came from the words within and under. Beyond their immediate denotation, his words have a connotative authority. The outer and inner meaning. In matching hues of blues, greens and golden browns, he painted a landscape, resplendent in motion and form. Though words can have power and the simultaneous lack of it, the intoxicating beauty was not lost on those who listened. For them, his word was the spark that set the world ablaze. They opened a space where anything is possible. Shining, radiant as the brightest star. He was a poet.

## MORNING LIGHT

*For Lynn Lupetti*

The woods mourn the day,
mindful not to stir
ghosts from the shadows,

as the bow glides
over strings
tuned in perfect fifths,

like a whispered prayer,
unaccountable sorrow,
a solitary voice,

branches tremble,
needles litter the ground,
deeply layered,

warm living tones, rich
vibrations resonate
in the morning light.

## AFTERLIFE

Slammed it shut, but he wedged his foot
in the doorway. He still hoped to find
breadcrumbs. If you slam a door on
someone you shut them out loudly. You
say, I can't do this anymore. I won't put
up with this, but when one door slams
another may open. He found himself in
a kind of afterlife, like a phantom limb,
a surviving ghost of a lesson. He languished
in the absence of closure. Is there life after
death? What follows the afterlife? A string
of harsh words, tears, regrets, anger, heavy
drinking, a year of no music, because every
song reminds him… Words lift off the page
inconsolable balloons tethered to circumstance.
He shaved his beard and found his
doppelgänger. Who is he now?

## IMMINENT SELF

There is a soul
weariness
that affects us all.

Where secrets swirl
and betrayals come
eventually.

Stop.

Unravel the strange
and inexplicable
blink of existence.

Be your own witness,
approval and disapproval,
equally meaningless.

Inhabit the silence,
create space
for new conversation.

Wait.

In *sweet darkness*,
mirror your own
unchanging heart.

The light of your face
is not lost
because of distance.

## END OF DARKNESS

A curved mouth
erupts in ironic laughter,
implies knowledge,
more than what is said.

Expansive gestures
portray an openness,
shifting eyes tell
another story.

A smug expression
smacks of judgement,
the forgotten capacity
for kindness.

Barbed wire demarcates
boundary, no one
crosses here.

Discordant words,
acrimony,
a single shutter
of remembrance.

## GENESIS OF BECOMING

Creation itself
is always in process.

With tongues of fire, tell me
something I don’t know.

Let revelation reveal a way
where there had been none.

Move forward in faith,
not delusional certainty.

Rest in the act of taking
the next step.

Uncharted, deep as mystery,
no middle, no binary extreme.

There is always more,
alternatively.

## THE RIVER'S EDGE

We walk barefoot on
polished stones, swift
currents past our ankles.

Water flows over pebbled
riverbed. Refracted light
glistens dreamlike.

We stay in the shallows
at the river's edge. A burning
noonday sun at our backs.

The harmonious stream
sings like a choir, rhythmic,
and continuous.

A gentle rush of water
trickles and gurgles
with occasional splash.

Ceaseless motion cycles
fresh rainwater between land,
ocean, and air.

The watercourse meanders,
nourishes life with every
twist and turn.

Each tributary carves and creates
habitat for wildlife, quenches
thirst of plants and trees.

In places, it's wide and deep.
We find a shallow spot, slow
enough to wade across.

Our steps ripple the braided
surface, fighting the undertow
of a faster cross-current.

In startled laughter—
you reach for my hand,
losing your balance.

## ONGOING ELEGY

In diffused porch light,
he fumbles with the lock,
bends down to pick up his
keys, curses under his breath.

Outside a neighbor's dog barks.
The heavy oak door creaks,
and curtains flutter with
his entrance.

In the stillness he feels like
a ghost caught in some other
life. He pours himself another
drink, raises the glass.

He hesitates, remembers the
caressing quality of her voice,
her soft full mouth, the mischief
in her eyes when she laughed.

Witness to his own annihilation, no
exact time frame for the neuropathy.
A penchant for punishment, a love
affair with suffering.

It feels like desire or like dying,
silence presses in from every corner.
Under a hideous moon his soul
lingers, sleep never comes.

## TERMINUS

*For Portia Hopkins*

Faces glow in candlelight,
in procession we walk
the distance.

*The labyrinth, a confusing*
*warren*, we must find our way
in and back out again.

Who measures the length,
width, and depth in which
all things live and exist?

The path forward,
even as a straight line
is never easy.

How can epigrammatic lives be
interpreted, when *from entrance*
*to altar* requires a lifetime?

## KEEPING FAITH

I first assented
to faith, with joy,
never having known
the disparity between
life and death,
heaven and hell,
belief and unbelief.

I held on to things
that got me through
before, following
a repetitive cycle,
hoping for a different
outcome, but streams
that ceased to flow
eventually dried up.

The mistaken need
for certainty and the
avoidance of doubt
reduced my faith to
irrational gimmickry.

Does conviction lead
us back to Eden or
only into constant
contention? You kept
insisting, there's no
consolation, religion
is a roller coaster
of ups and downs,
provisional at best.

Faith is that Sunday
suit, pressed and
starched, hung in a
closet, like something

newly purchased,
only to be laid out
in a coffin, buried
in the ground, to be
resurrected, to surface,
the submerged or lost
sense of wonder—
risen again.

## WONDER UPENDED

He was that kid who
spent much of his time
willing a cloak of
invisibility
around himself.

Caught up
in a restless state
between resistance
and submission, the need
for something concrete.

For want of approval,
to be that person
who hears and sees
what others
might overlook.

For fear of exposure,
the appearance
of failure,
he chased
perfection.

Never to consider
when trees lose
their leaves or how
a gentle wind can
change the moment.

## UNFINISHED

She had written a succession of unpolished
lines, printed posthumously, with all their
fits and starts, abandoned, cut short like the
life of the one who first put them down. She
believed in the singularity of things, marched
to a different drum. The life of an artist is never
finished. She was altogether lovely, a flaming
bonfire, the hissing echo of a violet burning.

## ACKNOWLEDGMENTS

By the end of 2020, the pandemic, California fires, political unrest and the continued loss of income had taken its toll on many of us. I found myself desperately needing distraction. Many people chose to create more art. For me this was beneficial, because I regularly worked from home making reproductions of other people's artwork. Although, this kept me busy while we all "sheltered in place," it was work, nonetheless. I found myself needing other outlets for dealing with the overwhelming circumstances.

For me that outlet became poetry. The poet Naomi Shihab Nye said, "I do think that all of us think in poems. I think of a poem as being deeper than headline news…otherwise, you just feel assaulted by all the tragedy in the world." Likewise, local poet and former U.S. Poet Laureate Ada Limón said, "It's so meaningful to lean on poetry right now because it does make you slow down. It does make you breathe." My poems are the result of that choice made six years ago. With the completion of this book arriving, I want to acknowledge the many people that have helped and inspired the writing of *Rattle of the Wind.*

I wish to thank Tamsin Spencer Smith and Matt Gonzalez for believing in my work and giving this book a home with FMSBW Press. I could not be more pleased with the professionalism and care they showed me while preparing this book for publication.

A heartfelt appreciation to Lehua M. Taitano, a CHamoru poet and artist who helped me with the initial copyediting of my poems and later assisted me with organizational/layout suggestions. Lehua encouraged me to take the editing process more seriously, insisting that it was where the "real magic happens."

My deepest gratitude to singer-songwriter, David Leon Zink. This book would not be possible without his friendship and guidance. I'm grateful for his having read my poems in their many permutations. His eye for typos and his generous suggestions were an inducement to my continued work on them.

A long overdue thanks to Jessica Berry, an artist, poet and novelist who read many of my earliest poems and provided feedback and support for my writing. I'm grateful for the many articles she sent and the discussions they brought about.

Many thanks to my beta readers, Kevin Kistler and Portia Hopkins, who provided thoughtful and essential feedback. Their academic and personal opinions both written and verbal, gave me courage to complete this project.

A special thanks to Robin Eschner, a painter and composer who years ago, invited me to sing with the Occidental Community Choir and currently with the Acorn MusEcology Project. She honored me by composing my poem, *Just Drive* into an amazing choral piece that has been performed in multiple concert programs. I can't read the poem without hearing her beautiful music. I am forever in her debt for this gracious gift.

I want to acknowledge my friends on social media, many that I know, some I have never met personally. The "likes" I received online were very affirming. So many of the "comments" were sincere and thoughtful. These were my first readers.

Finally, all my thanks to my wife Erin, her love and patience have supported me always. Honestly, she captured my heart the first time I saw her. Her creative spirit still inspires, and her writing advice continues to be invaluable.

*Darren Briggs*
*Sebastopol, CA*

## NOTES

My Antinomian Heart: The phrases “cut off the branches” and “golden ending” are taken from the world of role-playing video games. Cut off the branches refers to limiting the optional plot lines that a game might have. A golden ending or true ending is usually considered the final or best ending. The italicized words “Just as I am” are the title of a church hymn written by Charlotte Elliott in 1835, often sang during an alter call.

A Morning Walk: Earth Day, April 22, 2022.

Just Drive: Written December 24, 2021 and later composed into a song by Robin Eschner. First performed as a choral piece by the Acorn MusEcology Project on New Years Day 2023.

After the Rain: New Year’s Eve 2020. The italicized phrase “and I am waiting for a rebirth of wonder” is from Lawrence Ferlinghetti’s poem, *I Am Waiting* in his book, *A Coney Island of the Mind.*

Pictures of Jupiter: Prompted by the photos NASA released of Jupiter.

A Tender Mercy: The title of this poem was inspired by the movie, *Tender Mercies.* The line, “I never did trust happiness” is a paraphrased quote from the movie, delivered by actor Robert Devall. The phrase, “the appearance of everything is altered” is from William James, *The Varieties of Religious Experience*, where he quotes Jonathan Edwards’ description of his conversion.

Lazarus Reclining: The italicized phrase, “life’s inevitable contingency” is from Arthur W. Frank’s book, *The Wounded Storyteller.* In Susan Sontag’s essay, *Illness is Metaphor,*

“Illness is the night side of life, a more onerous citizenship. Everyone who is born holds dual citizenship, in the kingdom of the well and in the kingdom of the sick.”

Into the Mystery: The expression, “hour of shining stars” is from Walt Whitman’s, *Leaves of Grass* poem, *Pent-Up Rivers.* I wrote this poem the day after my brother, Terry Briggs passed away. February 2, 1958 - July 15, 2021

The Injury: The italicized phrase “geography is fate” is a quote from American writer, literary critic, and scholar Ralph Ellison’s 1979 speech at Brown University. In his novel *Invisible Man,* he wrote, “If you don’t know where you are, you probably don’t know who you are.”

War by Proxy: The Office of the United Nations High Commissioner for Human Rights (OHCHR) verified a total of 6755 civilian deaths during Russia's invasion of Ukraine as of December 11, 2022. Of them, 424 were children. Furthermore, 10,670 people were reported to have been injured. However, OHCHR specified that the real numbers could be higher.

Reading Kierkegaard: The italicized line “sorrow… on the verge of revelation” is borrowed from a comment in poet, Christian Wiman’s memoir, *Zero at the Bone.*

Perpetual Winter: Inspired by T. S. Eliot and Emily Hale’s hidden love affair. She was his “Hyacinth Girl” in *The Waste Land.* “Into the rose garden [their] words echo…” He wished to “inhabit” the memory of being together in *Burnt Norton* in the *Four Quartets*. Eliot wrote Hale over a thousand letters that were sealed in boxes “bound with steel” bands and held in the literary archives at Princeton University. The boxes of letters were opened Jan. 2, 2020, more than sixty years after Eliot’s death.

Where the Mind Goes: In loving memory of my brave mother, Marylane (Kitty) Briggs. February 1, 1935 - January 30, 2023

The Devil I Know: The first book referenced is *Bel-Ami,* by novelist Guy de Maupassant. The quote is not from the book but was my impression of the lead protagonist. The phrase "fake it till you make it" is a popular colloquialism. The Haruki Murakami quote is taken from *South of the Border, West of the Sun*. The Wendell Berry quote is from, *Life is a Miracle*. The T.S. Eliot reference is to his poem, *The Waste Land.* Franz Kafka's, "man on the bridge" is a reference to his short story, *The Judgment.* This is a devastating tale about a father who pushes his son to commit suicide. Following this is the true story of French philosopher and novelist, Albert Camus' death in a friend's speeding car. His views contributed to the rise of the philosophy known as absurdism. I alluded to two different Fyodor Dostoyevsky stories, *The Idiot* and *Crime and Punishment* to confuse things further. I quoted novelist Sally Rooney's, *Beautiful World* because I love everything she writes. The Ernest Hemingway quote is from the novel, *The Sun Also Rises*. The Samuel Beckett quote, "Fail again, Fail better" is from a short piece of prose entitled, *Worstward Ho!* The full quote reads, "Ever tried. Ever failed. No matter. Try again. Fail again. Fail better." The last quote attributed to Hunter S. Thompson is fictional.

Morning Light: For my dear friend Lynn Lupetti, in response to the memory of a conversation we had over dinner, when she excitedly described her ideas for a painting of instrumentalist, Edwin Huizinga playing his violin in the redwoods.

Imminent Self: This poem was inspired by my first reading of David Whyte's book, *House of Belonging*. The italicized words, "sweet darkness" are borrowed from the title of his famous poem.

Terminus: This poem borrows heavily from the language/symbols of the Church and my reading of Margret Visser's book, *The Geometry of Love*. The labyrinth, a symbol of change and transformation, represents our passage through mystery and meaning. Unlike a maze that may have multiple ways, a labyrinth leads to a certain endpoint. For this reason, I chose the title, Terminus. Margret describes the labyrinth as a "confusing warren," or in other words a rabbit hole. In the concluding line, Margret's phrase, "from entrance to altar" denotes the space, time and spiritual wisdom necessary, even to begin to unravel the significance of our lives. This "path forward" is historically symbolized by the center aisle in the architecture of most churches and represents life's journey.

*Darren Briggs, 2026*

**Darren Briggs** (he/him) is a poet based in Northern California. His work explores some of the pleasures and frailties of life, spirituality and nature. He is an avid reader and enjoys singing in a community choir. He holds a bachelor's degree in business leadership and theology. Darren has worked in the graphics industry for over forty-three years. Currently, he is owner of a printing company where he combines his technical expertise with his love for art and photography in the fine art printing industry. Darren is most often inspired by a deep connection to the natural world. *Rattle of the Wind* is his debut collection.

## THE PAGE POETS SERIES

Number 1
*Between First & Second Sleep* by Tamsin Spencer Smith

Number 2
*The Michaux Notebook* by Micah Ballard

Number 3
*Sketch of the Artist* by Patrick James Dunagan

Number 4
*Different Darknesses* by Jason Morris

Number 5
*Suspension of Mirrors* by Mary Julia Klimenko

Number 6
*The Rise & Fall of Johnny Volume* by Garrett Caples

Number 7
*Used with Permission* by Charlie Pendergast

Number 8
*Deconfliction* by Katharine Harer

Number 9
*Unlikely Saviors* by Stan Stone

Number 10
*Beauty Will Be Convulsive* by Matt Gonzalez

Number 11
*Displacement Geology* by Tamsin Spencer Smith

Number 12
*The Public Sound* by Marina Lazzara

Number 13
*Record of Records* by Rod Roland

Number 14
*Strangers We Have Known* by John Briscoe

Number 15
*Cutting Teeth* by Jesse Holwitz

Number 16
*Other Scavengers* by Lauren Caldwell

Number 17
*Cueonia* by Jesse Holwitz

Number 18
*In the Museum of Hunting and Nature* by Cynthia Randolph

Number 19
*A New Species of Color* by Tamsin Spencer Smith

Number 20
*Busy Secret* by Micah Ballard

Number 21
*Out of the Blue* by Fran Carbonaro

Number 22
*Broadway Azaleas* by Sunnylyn Thibodeaux

Number 23
*War News II* by Beau Beausoleil

Number 24
*Hailstones* by Justin Robinson

Number 25
*Exile on Beach Street* by Kevin Opstedal

Number 26
*Everyday Villanelles* by Kevin Arnold

Number 27
*Uncollected Poems* by Micah Ballard

Number 28
*At Dusk* by Fran Claggett-Holland

Number 29
*Rattle of the Wind* by Darren Briggs

THE DIVERS COLLECTION

Number 1
*Hôtel des Étrangers,* poems by Joachim Sartorius translated from German by Scott J. Thompson

Number 2
*Making Art,* a memoir by Mary Julia Klimenko

Number 3
*XISLE*, a novel by Tamsin Spencer Smith

Number 4
*Famous Dogs of the Civil War*, a novel by Ben Dunlap

Number 5
*Now Let's See What You're Gonna Do,* poetry by Katarina Gogou translated from Greek to English by A.S. with an introduction by Jack Hirschman

Number 6
*Sunshine Bell / The Autobiography of a Genius, an annotated edition* by Ben Dunlap

Number 7
*The Profound M: found photos paired with poems* by Tamsin Spencer Smith with an introduction by Matt Gonzalez

Number 8
*The Glint in a Fox's Eye & Other Revelations*, volume one of a three-part memoir by Ben Dunlap

Number 9
*The Origins of Bliss,* volume two of a three-part memoir by Ben Dunlap

Number 10
*Proud, Open-Eyed and Laughing*, volume three of a three-part memoir by Ben Dunlap

Number 11
*Esmerelda's Story,* a historical novella by Mary Julia Klimenko

Number 12
*Private Instigator, a Journey through the Underworld of Disorganized Crime* by Steve Vender

Number 13
*Dreaming as One, Poetry, Poets and Community in Bolinas, California 1967-1980* by Kevin Opstedal

Number 14
*Art Writings: 2008-2024* by Matt Gonzalez

Number 15
*Joey Chestnut's America: Politics, Patriotism and the Future of Democracy by* William W. Sokoloff

Number 16
*My California*, poems by Beau Beausoleil and paintings by Tamsin Spencer Smith

www.ingramcontent.com/pod-product-compliance
Lightning Source LLC
LaVergne TN
LVHW090533110826
845146LV00003B/1077

* 9 7 9 8 9 9 2 1 5 9 4 9 3 *